COLOUR AND ... ABOUT GOD

GOD IS EVERYWHERE

God is everywhere

He is with us when we are playing and having fun. "Do not I fill heaven and earth? declares the Lord." Jeremiah 23:24.

God

— — — —

everywhere

— — — — — — — — — — —

heaven

— — — — — —

Page 2 Key Words:

God

everywhere

heaven

God is everywhere

He is with us when we are in trouble and feel unhappy "When you pass through the waters I will be with you; and when you pass through the rivers, they will not sweep over you." Isaiah 43:2

with

— — — —

trouble

— — — — — — —

unhappy

— — — — — — —

Page 4 Key words:

with

trouble

unhappy

Go over the words you have learnt so far:

God
everywhere
heaven
with
trouble
unhappy

God is everywhere

We cannot hide from God. He always knows where we are. "You know when I sit and when I rise... You are familiar with all my ways." Psalm 139:2-3

knows

— — — — —

where

— — — — —

when

— — — —

Go over the words you have learnt so far:

God everywhere heaven with trouble unhappy knows where when

God is everywhere

He looks after us when we go to sleep at night and when we are awake.
"I lie down and sleep; I wake again, because the Lord sustains me."
Psalm 3:5

looks

— — — — —

sleep

— — — — —

awake

— — — — —

Page 8 Key words:

looks

sleep

awake

Go over the words you have learnt so far:

God	knows
everywhere	where
heaven	when
with	looks
trouble	sleep
unhappy	awake

God is everywhere

He is with us when we worship him in church or at home. "For where two or three come together in my name, there am I with them."
Matthew 18:20

worship

— — — — — — —

church

— — — — — —

home

— — — —

Page 10 Key words:

worship

church

home

Go over the words you have learnt so far:

God	knows	worship
everywhere	where	church
heaven	when	home
with	looks	
trouble	sleep	
unhappy	awake	

God is everywhere

No matter where we are, God can see us. He has promised to be with us always. "I am with you always, to the very end."
Matthew 28:20

see

— — —

promised

— — — — — — — — —

always

— — — — — —

Page 12 Key words:

see

promised

always

Go over the words you have learnt so far:

God	knows	worship
everywhere	where	church
heaven	when	home
with	looks	see
trouble	sleep	promised
unhappy	awake	always

These are all the words that you have learnt in this book. Try and fit them into the gaps in the following story to see how well you have learnt them.

	trouble	looks	home
God	unhappy	sleep	see
everywhere	knows	awake	promised
heaven	where	worship	always
with	when	church	

Did you know that __ __ __ is __ __ __ __ __ __ __ __ __ __?

He is in __ __ __ __ __ __ above and in the earth beneath. God

will always be __ __ __ __ us. He is even with us when we are

in __ __ __ __ __ __ __. He is with us when we are happy.

He is with us when we are __ __ __ __ __ __ __. God always

__ __ __ __ __ __ __ __ __ __ you are. He knows __ __ __ __

you are being good or being bad. God __ __ __ __ __ after us

all the time. He looks after us when we __ __ __ __ __.

He looks after us when we are __ __ __ __ __. Do you speak

to God? God is with us when we __ __ __ __ __ __ __ him and

tell him how wonderful and amazing he is.   We can worship

God when we are in __ __ __ __ __ __ or we can worship him

when we are at __ __ __ __. We can worship God everywhere

and anywhere. God can __ __ __ us wherever we are. He

sees everything. He has __ __ __ __ __ __ __ __ that he will

be with us __ __ __ __ __ __.